The Calling and Biblical Role of the Associate Minister

"God's Servant, Doing God's Work, God's Way, By God's Power"

Dr. Bernard P. Goode

REJOICE
Essential Publishing

Dr. Bernard P. Goode/Rejoice Essential Publishing

PO BOX 512

Effingham, SC 29541

www.republishing.org

Unless otherwise indicated, scripture is taken from the King James Version.

Scripture quotations marked (NIV) are taken from the Holy Bible, New International Version®, NIV®. Copyright © 1973, 1978, 1984, 2011 by Biblica, Inc.™ Used by per-mission of Zondervan. All rights reserved worldwide. www.zondervan.com The "NIV" and "New International Version" are trademarks registered in the United States Patent and Trademark Office by Biblica, Inc.™

Author's website:
www.youthfullyinspired4realministries.com

The Calling and Biblical Role of the Associate Minister/ Dr. Bernard P. Goode

ISBN-10: 1-946756-71-7
ISBN-13: 978-1-946756-71-8

"LORD, HERE I AM, SEND ME"

Isaiah 6:8 (KJV)

TABLE OF CONTENTS

Dedication

This book is dedicated to Pastor Laurie T. Adams for being a great inspiration and encourager in my life and ministry. This book is dedicated to Mt. Salem Baptist Church and all the men and women of God who serves in the gospel ministry as Servants Leaders of Jesus Christ. It is dedicated to my beloved spiritual father Dr. A. Lincoln James, Jr. pastor of the Trinity Baptist Church, Richmond, VA.

This book is dedicated to the following mentors: the late Dr. T Wright Morris (past president of Baptist General Convention), the late G.E. Patterson, (the presiding bishop of the Church of God in Christ), the late D. J Ragland, (Director of Virginia University of Lynchburg), Dr. A Lincoln James, Jr (Past President of Virginia State Baptist Convention and Vice Pres. National Baptist Convention Congress of Christian Education), Dr. Virgil Woods (Civil Rights Activist/ Martin Luther King, Jr) Dr. Henry Mitchell (Academic Dean/ Samuel DeWitt Proctor School of Theology) and Bishop Neil C. Ellis (Presiding Prelate of Global United Fellowship).

This book is also dedicated to the following ministers' license or ordained under the leadership and anointing of my ministry: Apostle James O. Smith, Prophetess Dinah Smith, Apostle William Winston, Pastor Robin Winston, Pastor Kevin Childs, Pastor Devon Edwards, Pastor Dr. Barbara Nollie, Pastor Wesley Tolliver, Pastor Nathaniel Scott, Minister LaShay Childs, Minister Frances McDuffie, Minister Alicia Croston, Minister Shelia Ross, Minister William Fells, Minister Vivian Woolfolk, Minister Delois Ferguson, Minister Edward Woolfolk, Elder Subremia Johnson, Prophet Kevin Smith. and Minister Jeryl Childs.

This book is dedicated to the following men-torees: Pastor Arthur Washington, Pastor Dr. Greg Beasely, Pastor Claybon Collins, Prophet Kevin Smith, and Minister William H. Fortune.

And above all, this book is dedicated to my Lord, Jesus Christ and His abounding grace.

Introduction

As I began to write this awesome book, I want to assure you as a reader that this book will change your life and view of the Calling and Biblical Role of the Associate Minister. The purpose of this book is to unveil and answer some of the important questions the associate minister will encounter regarding the call and role in ministry. I have been given the task to convey this topic from a theological and Biblical perspective. I have been assigned by God to share with the 21st century church a balanced view of the Biblical role of the associate minister. This book is designed to help you develop a right philosophy of ministry as you embark on the journey of self discovery as to what God is calling you to do in His kingdom.

Some of you will be transitioning from the ministry of an associate minister to the ministry of pastor; this book will enable you to teach potential sons and daughters who will be birthed under your anointing and leadership into the gospel ministry. Unlike many other books that have been very beneficial to your spiritual development, this book will escort you to the core of your calling as well as provide you with a clear, concise, and coherent understanding of the Biblical role of an associate minister. It will also teach you some insights regarding evangelism as it apply to the 21st century church.

The Ecclesiastical guidelines in this book are offered to help the pastor and associate minister establish and maintain an effective relationship within the Body of Christ. While every situation is different, it is important that the pastor communicate with the associate minister what is expected in their relationship. It is my prayer this book will bring spiritual transformation by revitalizing a renewed since of purpose in your calling as you are guided by the Holy Spirit to do the will of God in His church.

CHAPTER ONE

The Theological Starting Point for Ministry

UNDERSTANDING GOD'S CALL FOR MINISTRY

God calls people. *In Courage and Calling*, Gordon T. Smith claims that whether it is the calling of Abraham to leave the land of Ur and go he knew not where, or the calling of Moses, confronted with the burning bush, or the calling of Isaiah who encountered the glory of God, or the calling of St. Paul to bring the gospel to the Gentiles, an awareness of call is both mysterious and powerful.[1] The call of God is a profound mystery. It begins with God's purpose and ends with God's mission for a human individual. It is a personal call, but bigger than the person. God's call comes direct from God's ministry. *In The Soul of Ministry*, Ray S. Anderson explains that there is no other way to say it, God's ministry is the revelation of God to humans called to get to know God's nature, purpose and power.[2] The ministry of God's calling is one of great conundrum. It is very interesting how God calls flawed people to share a word of hope and encouragement to a flawed world. Throughout scripture God is revealed as calling and using imperfect people for the sake of His mission. I never understood why Jesus called the individuals he did. He didn't call the popular, rich, famous or successful to further His ministry, but rather, the poor, broken and flawed. Jesus did not call the equipped, He equipped the called.

It is helpful to understand that the call of God in two distinct ways. Smith explains, first there is a call to be Christian. The God of creation invites us to respond to His love. This call comes through Jesus, who invites us to be His disciples and to know the Father through Him. Second, for each individual there is a specific call-defining purpose or mission, a reason for being.[3] Paul the apostle explains that Jesus gave some apostles; prophets; evangelists and some pastors and teachers (Ephesians 4:11). Each ordinary person has a unique calling to do extraordinary things in the kingdom of God as it relates to the work of ministry.

WHO DOES GOD CALL FOR MINISTRY?

The theological starting point is the most crucial point for ministry. It is at this point that there must be a sound understanding and a right philosophy of ministry. It has once been asked by a group of Christians "who" does God call for the work of the ministry?

When looking at "who" does God call for the work of the ministry, some un-apologetically would say men are the only ones called into the gospel ministry, thus dismissing women from being called into the ecclesiastical status of the ministry. The foundation of this claim centers around a person's gender, whereas when God calls a person into the gospel ministry, Scripture teaches us that God does not look at our outward appearance (gender), but at our heart (Isaiah 16:7b).[4]

If this assertion is to be true, then the qualifying element in a person's calling for a sympathetic service in the gospel ministry is not gender, but the person must be Christ – like, belonging to Christ or a Christian possessing a servant's heart. Therefore, the starting point for ministry begins with salvation, being saved or redeemed by the grace of God.

Sad to say, some people have a misunderstanding between the call for salvation with the call for ministry. As a result of this mix-up, there are individuals who lay claim to be called into the gospel ministry, when what appeared to be their second calling for ministry is their initial calling for salvation. The quality must go in before the title goes on. Before a person becomes a preacher of the gospel, he or she must first be born-again or a Christian.

Illustration:

There are times when some parents are sincerely wrong regarding salvation and baptism. They are sincere in thinking their child need to be saved, but wrong in thinking baptism is the only essential element to the saving of one's soul; therefore, all my children will be baptized. It is upon this belief that some children are coerce by their parents to respond to the pastor's invitation to discipleship.

Jesus clearly explains in John12:32 that the call for salvation involves being "drawing" to Christ. *"And I, if I be lifted up from the earth, I will draw all men unto me.* [5] This drawing is done through the agency of the Holy Spirit's ability to convict and convince a sinner that he or she needs a Savior.

This is why the people of God are asked in 2nd Peter 1:10, "Wherefore the rather, brethren, give diligence to make your calling and election sure: for if ye do these things, ye shall never fall.[6] Peter urges believers to make their calling and election sure by understanding the call of salvation. Whenever, the calling for salvation is confused with the calling of ministry, one cannot walk worthy of the vocation by which he or she is called

(Ephesians 4:1).[7] In other words, your mind will lead you where your character can't keep you. It is hard to live right when you didn't get saved right. When the call for ministry is actually a call for salvation, the respondent, should be working out his or her soul salvation, instead of making full proof of the ministry. The call of salvation is the foundation for the call into the gospel ministry. It is at this point the associate minister or Christian enters into a relationship with the Holy Spirit. Whenever, the call for salvation is confused for the call into ministry, the respondent depends and operates off of oratorical or rhetoric skills which are often developed through theological training instead of the anointing of Jesus Christ. Jesus explains in Luke 4:18 he was anointed to preach the gospel. [8]

What does this mean? What are the characteristics of spirit-anointed preaching? Spirit-anointed preaching begins with the Holy Spirit and ends with the preacher. God does not anoint programs, eloquence, or education, but people, who have been equipped in collaboration with God to be entrusted with the power of the spirit.

Preaching that produces results, holds the attention of congregations, edifies churches, and glorifies God, is spirit-anointed preaching. It was this kind of preaching which characterized John the Baptist, Peter, Paul, John and Jesus. At Nazareth Jesus was invited to read the Scripture and then to preach. He read, "The Spirit of the Lord is upon me, because He hath appointed me to preach. One cannot preach the Good News without being anointed. The God, who calls us to preach, calls us to spirit-anointed preaching.

The anointing brings balance in preaching. In "*Be Quoted*," Warren W. Wiersbe explains that preaching must be marked by three elements: conviction, warning, and appeal ("reprove, rebuke, exhort"). To quote an old rule of preachers, "He should afflict the comfortable and comfort the afflicted." If there is conviction but no remedy, we add to the people's burdens. And if we encourage those who ought to be rebuked, we are assisting them to sin. Biblical preaching must be balanced.[9]

When looking through the eyes of the New Testament Scripture nothing holds greater priority or primacy than being anointed to preach. Churches who recognize and accept the importance of the centrality of being anointed to preach as a means of saving the lost, nurturing and inspiring the saved, and providing preventive maintenance against apostasy. Well-fed, stable, biblically literate congregations, who are growing in Christ, are often the products of the anointing which motivates people to become involved in sharing the benefits which they are receiving.

When the preacher recognizes the "anointing" as being the influence or power source in preaching, this prevents the preacher from developing spiritual pride. In other words, it prevents the preacher from getting puffed up with an over rated opinion of self and seduced and deceived by Satan that he or she is self- sufficient in the art of preaching. Warren W. Wiersbe claims that Satan's desire is to work in the local church, to hinder its ministry; and to do this he must work in and through Christians or professed Christians who are part of that fellowship. Pride is one of his chief weapons.[10] If he can get a pastor (preacher) proud of his preaching, a Sunday school teacher proud of his class's growth or a church officer proud of his experience and leadership, then Satan has a foothold from which to launch his attack. Pride opens the door to every other sin, for once we are more concerned with our reputation than our character, there is no end to the things we will do just to make ourselves "look good" before others. [11]

The associate minister when called by God and anointed to preach the gospel of Jesus Christ is anointed to preach the "Good News" boldly. Paul asked for prayer from his fellow believers that in preaching, he may have the right words, as he boldly tells others about the Lord (Eph 6:19-20). [12] The truth of God's Word ought to be preached boldly. If a man or woman is convinced of truth, he or she ought to preach it boldly and not proudfully, but with humility. If the listening audience is to see Jesus in preaching, humility will cause the preacher to disappear

In Expository Thoughts on the Gospel, J.C. Ryle argues that a faithful minister will never allow anything to be credited to him, or his office, which belongs to his divine Master. He will say like Paul, "We preach not ourselves, but Christ Jesus, the Lord, and ourselves your servants for Jesus' sake." (2 Cor. 4:5.) To commend Christ dying, and rising again for the ungodly–to make known Christ's love and power to save sinners, this will be the main object of his ministry. "He must increase but I must decrease," will be a ruling principle in all his preaching. He will be content that his own name be forgotten, so long as Christ crucified is exalted. Therefore, humility is the right understanding of who you are before God.

When Jesus Christ washed his disciple's feet in John Chapter 13, he was teaching the disciples a lesson in humility. He wanted his disciples then and now to understand that there are times when the minister must drop the title and pick up the towel and go into the repulsive and distasteful areas of life and demonstrate the depth of humility toward all people in all circumstances, whether they are faithful or unfaithful.

Andrew Murray proposes that our relationship with God and man is made visible by a penetrating humility. Without humility, there can be no true dwelling in God's presence or enjoying His favor and the power of His Spirit.[14] Humility is simply the expression of nothingness, which comes when a person see how God is all in every aspect in life. Wilkes maintains that humility, not pride, is the hallmark of a minister's character. Associate ministers must humble themselves and wait for God to exalt them. Humility cannot be forced. Humility comes from the center of a person—from integrity and honesty. A true minister of God is one who can essentially stay out of the way, whose ego is not at the center, but the periphery of the work of God.

CHAPTER TWO

The Theological Foundation for Ministry

WHAT KIND OF PERSON DOES GOD CALL FOR MINISTRY?

The theological root of God's call for ministry goes back to the prophetic tradition of Israel. The prophetic image of the call is not rooted in perfection, but it is based on God's transformation of a person who has been broken into being a wounded healer.

In The Wounded Healer, Henri Nouwen persists that the call of Isaiah illustrates what the call means for the wounded healer. In Isaiah 6:1-13, the prophet's call includes announcing his brokenness, wounded-ness and vulnerability, to which an angel of the Lord attends. The prophet declares of himself: "And I said: "Woe is me! For I am a man of unclean lips, and I dwell in the midst of a people of unclean lips; for my eyes have seen the King, the Lord of hosts!" (Isaiah 6:5)

The same is accurate in Jeremiah 1:4-9, where Jeremiah felt unfit to be a prophet because as a youth with little experience he felt defenseless. In verse 6, he says: "Ah, Lord God! Behold, I do not know how to speak, for I am only a youth." The prophet Moses was also reviewed as broken, wounded and vulnerable in the book of Exodus. In being called, Moses found that God gave him words to prepare him for the task.

In Isaiah chapters 41 – 43, we have a clear, concise, and coherent picture of the "call" and it's implications for carrying out ministry. God promises encouragement to theses servants as they perform God's call. God promises to empower, and enable them in their work. God also promises to give them His spirit so that they can complete their assign task. Careful examination of the call emphasizes fact that God's call involves those who were not perfect, but inadequate and insecure.[16]

THE NATURE OF THE CALL

In this chapter, we will examine the nature of the calling. In Hebrews 5:4 we are told that "...no man takes this honor (of spiritual leadership) unto himself, but he that is called of God." In other words, no man can be a preacher of the gospel of Jesus Christ just because he wants to be. He has to be called by God and sent by God. In Paul's Epistles, he always opens by referring to himself as "an apostle of Jesus Christ by the will of God." He recognized that his ministry came not from his own personal ambitions or ideas, but through the sovereign will of God.

Romans 1:1 gives us even further detail: "Paul, a servant of Jesus Christ, called to be an apostle..." Take particular notice of the word "called." The Greek word used is "kletos," which means "invited." The ministry is by invitation only. You can not invite yourself. James 3:1 further tells us "...be not many masters (teachers), knowing that we shall receive the greater condemnation." In other words, God will judge ministers by a stricter standard than He will judge lay people, so we should not even desire to enter the ministry unless we know that the call is there.

God's call to ministry cannot be manufactured. In Mastering the Pastoral, Cedar, Huges, and Patterson explains that "A call has no maps, no itinerary to follow, no destination to envision. Rather, a call depends upon hearing a Voice. [17] There are two calls to ministry: the inward and the outward call. The purpose of the inward or internal call to ministry serves as an introduction of the Divine presence of God. If God has called you, He will enable you, enlighten you, equip you, and encourage you.

The purpose of the outward or external call to ministry, on the other hand, is to examine and confirm the preliminary intuitions of an inward call by deliberately testing and assessing a candidate's potential for service to the body of Christ.

ANSWERING THE CALL

Once the minister accepts his or her calling, the following consideration must be given regarding Education. The Bible teaches us the only weapon the devil can use against the church is ignorance (Being untrained, unaware and misinformed about God). God said in Hosea 4:6, "My people are destroyed for a lack of knowledge." [18]

The first ministry of the church is teaching. This is why Jesus told his disciples (students, pupils, and learners) in the Great Commission, "Go ye therefore, and teach all nations, baptizing them in the name of the Father, and the Son, and of the Holy Spirit. Teaching them to observe all things whatsoever I have commanded you: (Matthews 28:19-20).[19] When we look at God's Servant, Doing God's Work, In God's Way, By God's Power, the first ministry of the Holy Spirit is teaching. "But the Comforter, which is the Holy Ghost, whom the Father will send in my name, he shall teach you all things (John 14:26). [20]

Therefore, if the first ministry of the church and the Holy Spirit is to be teaching, then the first ministry of the associate minister is to be learning. In Paul's second letter to Timothy, he instructs Timothy to "study or learn as one approved unto God, a workman that needs not be embarrassed as a person who correctly handles the word of truth. This charge is for all Christians and especially for us who have been called to the gospel ministry. Just as we expect our medical doctors and lawyers to be fully trained, educated, and certified, the people of God are worthy of the same level of expertise. We must provide the waiting congregation with the same level of competence and certification.

WHY GO TO SEMINARY?

I have discovered that there are two essential reasons why members of the cloth should attend Bible College or seminary. The first reason is to increase one's knowledge. A Bible College or seminary training should add a new dimension in the overall fund of Bible knowledge necessary for the ministry today.

Knowledge of Biblical languages is a must if we really believe in the verbal inerrancy of the Scriptures. Because the Bible has but one unified, coherent network of truth, an ignorance of systematic theology is not only tragic but unforgivable. Due to the higher education level of people in one's ministry context, along with the ever increasing tide of good Biblical scholarship, today's minister must be well prepared to keep abreast of Biblical studies to meet modern man on his own intellectual level with the truth of the Word of God. No amount of self study, praying, hoping, or wishing can substitute for a thorough seminary education. Therefore, seminary training is designed to help the associate minister understand the people inside and outside the ministry context.

The second reason for seminary training is maturity, in several areas. Seminary training will greatly improve one's social and spiritual maturity, as well as his or her ability to understand and relate to people and their needs. Effective seminary training will do wonders for one's decision making ability as well as strengthening the minister's ability to discern the will of God through the usage of Scriptures as applied to a given situation. Too many ministers make life-altering decisions involving themselves, their families, and congregation on the basis of emotion (usually anger or frustration), and personal interest.

In 10 Things Every Minister Needs To Know, Ronnie Floyd argues that decision making is not about you. The challenge of decision making in ministry is the influence of the rising tides that surround us. We are pressured to make decisions due to specific situations. The persuasive argument is to make it relative to where you are in a given situation. We are pressured to make decisions due to our feelings. The pressure comes at this point both externally and internally, calling us to "feel" our way in decision making. We are pressured to make decisions that will lead to the greatest results.

Within our churches there are special interests groups who push or shove us, attempting to intimidate us into getting involved in every issue that comes down the pipeline, all in the name of obtaining their own desired results pertaining to the issue at hand. As ministers, we can get ourselves into some real trouble when we make our decisions in ministry based upon situations, feelings, or even desired results. As ministers we must be compelled to make decisions that are consistent, and best for everyone involved. Therefore, situations, feelings, and desired results cannot be the criteria. Decision can be right, consistent, and best when they are decisions that God desires. These decisions must be based upon the authority of Scripture. [21]

Finally, I urge members of the clergy not to sell themselves short with a bob-tailed preparation. Study the principles and implication of Proverbs 24:27, "Prepare thy work without, and make it fit for thyself in the field; afterwards build your house."[22] In other words, do nothing without a plan. Develop your business first before building your home.

Yes, the Holy Spirit guides and directs, but the more you give God to use, the more God can make of you. Paul wants us to understand that a soldier of Christ has to be willing to prepare himself/herself for full-fledged work in God's kingdom. With this in mind, we are expected to further our education for the cause of Christ to the highest possible level. There are many accredited and non-accredited schools, Bible Colleges, and seminaries in most cities, pray that the Holy Spirit will guide and direct you to the ministry of learning.

On the contrary, there are some self taught pastors and associate ministers who truly love the Lord Jesus Christ, yet they hold reservation about schools of theology. Some have taken what Paul said in 2nd Corinthians 3:6, *"The letter kills and the Spirit gives life"* to undermine theological training and denote seminaries as cemeteries.[23]

This phrase from 2nd Corinthians 3:6 is perhaps one of the most misused in New Testament Scripture. What is this passage saying? To understand this phrase we must first see it in context:

1) Historical Background;

From this context, we can clearly see that Paul is talking about false teachers who have been issuing 'letters of recommendation' and causing dissension in the church, to undermine his apostolic authority. When reading verse one, Paul stresses that the Corinthian themselves are his 'letter' of recommendation. Then in verse two, we are told that the holy community at Corinth was saved by his ministry through the Spirit writing of God's Word on their hearts. In verse three (3), the passage explains this is not due to Paul's cleverness or ability, but God's grace and promise found in the New

Covenant, that he would write His Word or Law on the hearts of His people by His Spirit thereby bringing them eternal life and forgiveness of sins.

The meaning of the phrase *"the letter kills, but the spirit gives life"* refers to the fact that under the Old Covenant, the law or letter given on Sinai brought condemnation and death as no one could obey it perfectly and be saved. However, now that Christ (the anointed one or messiah) has come and perfectly obeyed the Law as mediator for His people, the Spirit brings life by using the same 'letter' and writing into our hearts.

In other words, where the letter, law, and Word alone brings condemnation to the unregenerate person who rejects it, but when this same Word is accompanied by the work of the Holy Spirit in someone's heart, it brings life and salvation. Far from teaching that the Word and Spirit are opposed, this passage reaffirms the essential connection between the two.

THE SCHOOL IN THE WILDERNESS

Dr. Dave Earley the chairman of the Department of Pastoral Leadership for Liberty University and Liberty Theological Seminary, as well as author of *"21 Reasons Bad Things happen to Good people"* explains that often we have a mistaken view of what qualifies us to minister effectively to others. Education is certainly help-ful. Training is always good. Gifts are important. But we too often overlook the fact that it is in the loneliness of the wilderness and the difficulties of the desert that God truly prepares us to minis-ter to others.[24] In other words, God uses the wilderness for training ground; it is there that God teaches dependence, trust, and obedience.

Therefore, the first reason for training in the school of the wilderness is that out of our painful experiences we develop a deep desire to help others. In the classroom of suffering and sorrow, we learn the ministry of helping the hurting. When you have been down the same road of suffering as another, you can minister from your life story. When you have set where they set, a connection can be made. A relationship can be established and trust can be built. Then real ministry occurs. The very best person to help someone who is suffering is someone who has suffered.[25]

In seminary you learn about God's forgiveness and in the wilderness you experience God's forgiveness. Paul said where sin abounded, grace did much more abound (Romans 5:20b).[26] In other words, the more we see our sinfulness, the more we see God's abounding grace forgiving us.

Seminary teaches the student about conflict, the wilderness teaches the student when he is in conflict. In seminary the associate minister seeks to learn about God through the study of theology.

In seminary the associate minister learn to harness the power of positive thought. The school in the wilderness reminds the man or woman of God of their fragileness and humanness. It reminds the herald of the gospel of the need of the sufficient grace of God. The school in the wilderness is where the ambassadors of Christ develop a right philosophy of ministry. It is where the associate minister is taught a God honoring ministry, that it is not about us, but it is all about God and the righteousness of Jesus Christ. It is where the associate minister learns the difference between religious activity that promotes pride and arrogance and ministry that glorifies God.

In seminary the associate minister learns about faith. In the school of the wilderness, the associate minister develops his or her faith. There are two lessons the associate minister learns about faith in the wilderness. First, the associate minister learns that "Faith releases the power of God."

Illustration:

When the disciples in Matthews Chapter 17 had encounter the boy who was mentally deranged, and in great trouble, for he often was tempted or convinced by a evil spirit to commit suicide by falling into the camp fire or drowning in a nearby lake of water. The disciples were unable to cure the boy. So the disciples went to Jesus inquiring why they couldn't cast out the evil presence in this boy's life. Jesus replied it is because of your unbelief or lack of faith. Previous to this encounter, according to Luke Chapter 9:1, Jesus had already given His disciples the authority and power to heal the sick and cast out demons. In other words, they had the power, but didn't have the faith. They like some today, some believe in God, but don't believe God. Jesus had already given His disciples the authority and power to heal the sick and cast out demons. They had the power, but no faith to activate the power. God does trust his power to those who will not trust and have faith in him.

What is faith? Faith is having confidence in God. Faith means we trust His timing, we claim His promises, and we rest in His love.

Second, the associate minister learns that God responds to our "Faith." In Matthews Chapter 17, we are told that when the disciples were unable to cure the boy or cast out the evils spirits. The disciples and the boy had an unmet need. Scripture teaches us that the key to changing anything is faith. If you want to change your circumstance and situation, it takes faith. If you want to change anything in your life, you have to have some faith.

Jesus said in Matthew 9:29, "According to your faith it will be done to you." No one can release your faith but you. Listen to it again, "According to your faith it will be done to you." That means we tend to get out of life what we expect. Why? Because, Hebrews 11:1 teaches us "Now faith is the substance of things hoped for: In other words, faith must always be accompanied with expectation that something good is about to happen. You can not have true faith unless you expect to receive something from God because "Faith is the substance of things hoped for. It is the evidence of things not seen. I can't see it but I know it is there. I can't see this new job, but I know it is there. I can't see this new relationship, but I know it is there. I can't see my healing, but I know it is there.

Hebrews 11:3 teaches us, "By faith we understand that the worlds were framed by the word of God." In other words, God said it and it was. God said let there be light and it was light. When God spoke the word of faith, he expected something good to happen. When we speak the word of faith, it brings God directly into our situation and circumstances. The school in the wilderness teaches the associate minister that the key element in pleasing God is faith. Paul said "For without faith it is impossible to please Him: for he that cometh to God must believe that he is, and that he is a rewarder of them who diligently seek him.[27] In other words, the associate minister can never please God without faith and every act of ministry, preaching, tithing, worship, and prayer, the associate minister must do in faith.

In the school of the wilderness is where the associate minister learns how to trust God. Learning to trust is a process that develops gradually. It is like an infant that enters into the process of learning to walk. Sometimes the child falls down only to get back up and start all over again. The same is true with trust, sometimes the associate minister stumbles and fail, only to get back up and start all over again, learning to trust God.

When the associate minister takes his or her first step in trusting God in the wilderness, it is at this point that the associate minister learns that trust is a risk we take. The risk we take is that we let some part of our life go out of our control and place it into the hands of God. King David once said "Some trust in Chariots, and some trust in horses, but we will remember to trust in God (Psalms 20:7 NIV).[28] It is in the school of the wilderness that the associate minister learns that God is his or her source and not a resource.

In the book of Exodus at Chapter 15 and from verse 22, we learn that God didn't take the Children of Israel straight to the Promised Land. Yes, the Promised Land of milk and honey and blessing were there waiting for the people, but they had to travel to the land through the wilderness. In other words, the wilderness is pretty rough at times. It can be very barren, throwing up various dangers with tough and almost terrifying experiences. It doesn't matter where you are physically - by the pool and the palm trees of Elim - or beside the bitterly disappointing waters of Marah. Whatever, situation you are in, Jesus clearly explain, "Yes, I am the Vine; you are the branches. Whosoever lives in me and I in him shall produce a large crop of fruit. For apart from me you can't do a thing (John 15:5).[29] Therefore, the associate minister must acknowledge that God is the minister's source, without God he or she can do nothing. It is in the wilderness the associate comes to the end of self and see self only as a resource and not the source of your spiritual blessings. The wilderness grooms a total dependency upon God to supply our needs.

Some ministers today are wandering in the wilderness. Not sure why or where they are going next. Because of their religious teaching some feel as if they are being punished by God. Fear is driving them because of lack of vision. As a result they have grown cold and bitter and feel the Lord has forsaken them. They like the children of Israel they have fallen into doubt, unbelief, idolatry, jealousies, envies, sedition's, and lusts.

Others have learned how to worship God in the loneliness of the desert, only to find out that there are times when God simply puts us on hold to teach us an important lesson on patience. A good illustration can be seen from the following:

The story of Mary and Martha in John Chapter 11 reveals to us that there are times when God puts us on hold. The story tells us that Mary and Martha's brother, Lazarus was sick. The sisters expected Jesus to quickly respond to their need, after all Lazarus was the friend of Jesus, but the text said He did nothing for two days. Then Jesus took another two days to travel or get to Bethany. By now Lazarus had been dead for four days. In the interim, little did Mary and Martha realize that God had put them on hold? Like some ministers today, who are waiting or have been praying for God to work a miracle in their life or ministry and nothing has happen as of yet. It seems like the blessing has been held up, the promises of God has been delayed, put off, rescheduled, and at times postpone, only to find out there are times when God puts us on hold to begin the process of developing patience.

The first phase in the process of developing patience begins with the test of faith. Faith cannot be trusted unless it has first been tested. God tests our faith in the wilderness to produce patience. God wants us to trust his timing. James said: my brethren, count it all joy when ye fall into divers' temptations; knowing this, that the trying of your faith worketh patience. But let patience have her perfect work, that ye may be perfect and entire, wanting nothing (James 1:1-4 KJV).[30]

Why is it so hard to develop patience? One reason is that patience is contrary to our human nature. Patience is not something we are born with. When a baby wakes up in the middle of the night and is hungry or his diaper is wet, he doesn't lie there and think, "I know mom and dad are tired. So I'll just wait until a more convenient time to let them know that I need something to eat or my diaper changed." No that baby cries immediately because it wants attention now. We are not born patient. On the contrary, it's our nature to be impatient. We also struggle with patience because we live in a time of hurry. Our society is constantly in a hurry. Some of us are so used to living in the fast lane, we can't stand delays. Yet Proverbs 19:11 says, "Blessed is the wise man who learns to be patient."[31]

There are a number of very interesting definitions that people have come up with that may help us understand what patience is. Patience is the ability to put up with people you don't like. Patience is accepting a difficult situation without giving God a deadline to remove it. Patience is an inner calmness that comes from the knowledge that God is in control." The spiritual definition of patience is trusting in God's perfect timing. This is what Mary and Martha had to learn, "Trusting in God's perfect timing. Because we don't understand God's timing, we live upset and frustrated, wondering when God is going to do something. When you understand God's timing however, you won't live all stressed out. You can relax knowing that God is in control, and at the perfect time, He is going to make it happen. Scripture says, "The vision is for the appointed times, through it tarry, wait earnestly for it, for it will come to pass." [32] In other words, God sends nothing before it is ready.

God said, "For I know the plans I have for you," declares the Lord, "plans to prosper you and not to harm you, plans to give you hope and a future (Jeremiah 29:11).[33] " This Scripture reveals that God provides for us although there times we are unaware of what he is doing. God has a plan set in motion for us, a plan to bless us and not harm us. Therefore, we must trust in his perfect timing for he sends nothing before it is ready. So be patient and trust God.

THE WORD OF GOD CREATES THE RESPONSE

In the school of the wilderness is where the associate minister learns that the Word of God creates a response. There are ministers like Moses, who only learning experience will come from bleak and lonely landscape of Sinai wilderness. This does not disqualify them from being a minister that God can use, because the Word of God creates the response out of nothing. Ray S. Anderson explains that we have discovered Moses, a fugitive from Egypt, an outcast from Pharaoh's house, a sheepherder these past forty years. This the man who once had access to political and personal power but who lost it all in an impulsive act. He killed an Egyptian who was beating a Hebrew. [34] When Pharaoh discovered the deed, Moses fled for life in the wilderness of the desert (Ex. 2:11-15). Anderson persists that this is the man who turned aside to see the bush burned but was not consumed. This is the man who heard the voice of God call him out of a burning bush, thus making him the first theologian in the Bible. This is the man, a fugitive and failure, eighty years old, powerless and penniless, who God called to lead the Hebrews out of bondage and into the land of promise.[35] The inner logic of Moses's story, is that the Word creates the response out of nothing. Let us reflect on David in the pasture. As leader and king, David also excelled. Like Moses, his life combined intimacy with God formed in solitude, and strong leadership unexplainable except for the fact, the Word of God creates the response out of nothing. What I like most about the story of David, his security and success was not because of any accolades, talent, giftedness, or intellectual dexterity. It was not because he was a magnificent musician or poet, rather it was due to the fact the Word of God creates the response out of nothing.

David had no expertize in wrestling bears or how to bring down giants like Goliath. Yet he was able to take out bears and giants, it was all because the Word of God creates the response out of nothing. There is no record that David had any training. There is no record that David was enrolled in the school of the prophets, yet he was able to write seventy three psalms, including the most notable 23rd Psalms. There is no other explanation to David's story but the Word of God creates the response out of nothing.

Elijah in the desert: Like Moses, he was without any of the trappings of human power or influence. He too was a man of the desert. The first time we meet him in Scripture he announces that there will be neither dew nor rain except by his word. He was sent by God to challenge Ahab, the most evil king ever to reign in Israel, and his 400 priests of Baal. Elijah, virtually single-handedly, turned a rebellious Israel back to the God of their fathers. The anointing of God for great acts was the source of his power, born in intimacy with him, cultivated during years of solitude in the desert. The Word of God creates the response out of nothing.

The power of the word case studies above reveals that the Word creates the response out of nothing. The effects of God's word is produced from the word itself. When God speaks there is a response and that response comes from God's Word. Every response of God's Word occurs when the element of human possibility is removed. "Powerlessness" is itself a necessary ingredient in the divine chemistry in how God's Word creates a response. Why did the Lord wait until Moses was eight years old, a failure and fugitive, with no possibilities? The selection of the barren womb of Sarah represents the same powerlessness of Moses. God's Word responds when the element of human possibility is removed. Sarah is to bear a son who will become the heir through which the covenant promise is to be fulfilled. Abraham will have so many descendants that they can scarcely be counted, as many as the stars in heaven (Gen. 15:5 NIV). Scripture teaches "You have observed correctly," said the LORD, "for I am watching over My word to accomplish it" (Jer. 1:12 BSB). The same Word that brings a sentence of death is the same Word that creates the possibility of life. It is the barrenness of Sarah that catches our attention. Her inability to conceive is a formidable barrier to the realization of Abraham's dream but opportunity for the Word of God to create a response of nothing.

When ministers come to the end of themselves, they will see the beginning of God. This is not to denounce theological training but it is a profound truth that the Word of God creates the response out of nothing. It is good to educated, it is best to be educated from on high, it is better to be both.

CHAPTER THREE

The Biblical Role of the Associate Minister

NEW TESTAMENT

The church is a special group in the world with a primary task. The functions of the church are evangelism (to make Christians into disciples) and edification (to build up by teaching). These two functions answer two questions. First, why does the church exists in the world? And second, why does the church exist as a gathered Community? Understanding the answers gives the servant of Christ or the associate minister a "hold" on individual duty and responsibility as it is related to his or her Biblical role in the ministry of Jesus Christ.

In the article *A New Decade Demands A New Breed of Managers*, Harari and Mukai explains that the real difference in the performance of effective and ineffective leaders was not experience or motivation; but the accuracy of understanding one's role. How one *thinks* directly affects how one *performs*.[36] As the writer of Proverbs 23:7 indicated, *what one thinks in their heart is one of the greatest factors of understanding*, especially when perceiving one's roles in the ministry. I will attempt to identify the role of the associate minister from a Biblical perspective.

The clearest model of the role of the associate minister can be seen in the New Testament book of Ephesians Chapter 4:11 where Paul says "And God gave some to be "Evangelists" for the edifying (building up) of the body of Christ.[37] In other words, some of us have been given special ability as apostles, to others he has given the gift of being able to preach well; some have special ability in winning people to Christ, helping them to trust him as their Savior, still others have a gift for caring for God's people as a shepherd does his sheep, leading and teaching them in the ways of God.

In majority of cases there are times when some people in the church refer to the associate minister as being the "Pastor" of a church. This is a misuse of term. The community of believers in our day suffers from a confusion of tongues. The terms used in the Scriptures are often applied to those things which are foreign or alien to their original meaning, and new words have been coined to describe Biblical concepts which serve only to alter the Biblical meaning of the term associate minister.

For example, no where in the Old Testament or New Testament Scripture do you hear the terms "Associate Minister" and "Associate Pastor". Yet these terms are noble (Having or showing qualities of high moral character) among our religious practices in protestant churches. Moreover, there are times when these gracious terms deviates from its intended meaning of the term associate minister.

For one to attempt to recapture or recover the Biblical meaning attached to the term associate minister. This means the ecclesiastical ideas with which the term have been clothed must be revealed through the translation of Greek terms. A good illustration of what I mean is found in the word "minister."

"Minister" is from the Latin word ministro, which means "to serve, to attend, and to wait on." A minister is one who serves, and any service rendered is ministry.

The word "minister" designates one as a servant but never, of itself, expresses or suggests the kind of service rendered. One simply cannot tell by looking at the word, the nature of the service.

Illustration:

A pastor is a minister, but every minister is not a pastor, a priest is a minister, but every minister is not a priest. In spite of this, to speak of "the associate minister' in our day is to refer to only one functionary of the Clergy. In justification for this it is urged by the language that Paul declared in Ephesians 4:11, "And he gave some to be Evangelists. Consequently, the associate minister according to the book of Ephesians is an "Evangelist."

Paul, Christianity first theologian instructed Timothy to preach the word; be instant in season, out of season; reprove, rebuke, exhort with all longsuffering and doctrine (2nd Timothy 4:2). He also included, "But watch thou in all things, endure afflictions, do the work of an evangelist, make full proof of thy ministry (2nd Timothy 4:5).[39] But the central question being asked in this study is where has the evangelist gone? More and more I am recognizing that majority of the associate ministers or evangelists in the 21th century church want to be pastors. Some are called to be pastors and some simply want to be pastors. Some evangelist enjoy being behind the pulpit more than in the highway and hedges compelling people to come into the house of God through the ministry of evangelism.

The pastor and evangelist play a vital role in the growth of the church. The pastor has been anointed to focus on shepherding and teaching the people of God as they enter into the sheepfold. The natural tendency of the pastor is to focus on taking care of the sheep, being a good shepherd of the church flock. The associate minister or evangelist is anointed to focus on outreach as he or she prepares the hearts of people to enter into the sheepfold through a personal relationship with Jesus Christ. The natural tendency of the evangelist is to focus on outreach all the time, and this helps to keep the church focused on the Great Commission of Jesus Christ, going into the entire world and their community.

THE DEFINITION OF THE EVANGELIST

The office of evangelist has been ill defined. The different usage of the term has caused great confusion with our ecclesiastical body of churches. The word evangelist will be defined in this chapter, with some qualities of the evangelist. The evangelist's ministry is predominately a preaching ministry. Paul's admonition to Timothy was, *"preach the word; be instant in season, out of season; reprove, rebuke, exhort with all longsuffering and doctrine."* (II Timothy 4:2) The evangelist's preaching will be marked different from pastoral preaching while complimenting and reinforcing the pulpit ministry of the God-called pastor. The evangelist pulpit is the street corners, byways and highways where his or her message is a compelling message calling sinners to repentance.

The type of preaching common to the evangelist is peculiar to the evangelist alone. But the evangelist's work is not restricted to only preaching, though that is his primary ministry. He will be engaged in other ministry endeavors assisting in the growth and edification of the local churches he is privileged (not entitled) to minister in.

The evangelist is engaged in the ministry of pastoral support, coming alongside the pastor to assist him in the edification and the building up of the local church, working under the direct oversight of the pastor, never usurping his authority. As is the case with the pastor, the evangelist is in the business of feeding the sheep through the operation and administration of his particular spiritual gift.

The evangelist is specifically equipped for revival work as a "*specialty*." As with any spiritual gift, there are differences of administration, and diversities of operation (I Corinthians 12:4-7). The ministry of the evangelist is also a "stirring and awakening" ministry, it is a confrontational ministry. God has empowered, equipped and gifted him to stir and awaken God's people in a very definite and special way.

The gift of the evangelist or associate minister is strategic, it is planned, tactical, and premeditated in its importance. The evangelist influences, inspire, and encourage unity. He or she influences fellowship around the message of Christ. Evangelists have great influence on young and elderly people. They help people get their lives in order as they cry out in confession of sin and repentance. Evangelists indeed are encouragers. They have influence on pastors, and encourage and strengthen their hands to the work God has given them.

The evangelist stirs people to win souls. Their preaching brings men and women to a decision – a holy ultimatum. The evangelist is to have a burden for his nation, and particularly for revival in these last days. The evangelist must be a "weeping prophet" and a "prayer warrior" if he is to see his ministry bear fruit. He cries out of his brokenness and repentance in a dry and thirsty land. His is a "ministry-support" endeavor.

It is part of his ministry to give God's people a vision and passion for revival, for, "Where there is no vision, the people perish" (Proverbs

29:18). However, in our contemporary ministries the pastors and churches tend to call pastors to do the work of an evangelist. Yet the scripture teaches "And he gave some, apostles; and some, prophets; and some, evangelists; and some, pastors and teachers." Why? The evangelist functions in three areas: 1). for the perfecting of the saints, 2). for the work of the ministry, and 3). for the edifying of the body of Christ (Ephesians 4:11-12). The central question that is to be asked in this study is how can the evangelist perfect the saints, do the work of the ministry and edify the body of Jesus Christ? It can be done through training others in the area of evangelism!

When called and chosen by God to the divine duty of an evangelist, he or she is anointed to serve in the area of evangelism. When traveling the by ways and highways of life, the assignment of the evangelist anointing is to lift every burden and break every yoke. Isaiah 10:27 teaches us "The anointing shall lift every burden and shall destroy every yoke.[41]

Jesus who is known as the "Master Evangelist" validates the assignment of the anointing. Jesus said in Luke 4:18, "The Spirit of the Lord is upon me, because he hath anointed me to preach the gospel to the poor; he hath sent me to heal the broken hearted; to preach deliverance to the captives, and recovering of sight to the blind, to set at liberty them that are bruised.[42] In other words, the anointing will lift every burden and break every yoke. The anointing is designed to end the bondage of God's people.

The evangelist or associate minister is not a freelancer or lone ranger, but is under the authority of his or her sending pastor and church. He or she is sent out by the pastor and local church to help another pastor and local church. Of great importance to the ministry of the evangelist is to be a part of a local church where his ministry is understood, and the work of the evangelist is loved, encouraged and supported.

The evangelist must, by all means, have a strong bond and working relationship with his pastor. It is difficult to serve under a pastor not having a vision for the work of an evangelist and a burden for the revival ministry. The evangelist and pastor must be pulling together in the same harness, and must have a mutual burden and vision for the three-fold purpose of both pastor and evangelist (the perfecting of the saints – the work of the ministry – the edifying of the body of Christ).

There are too many evangelists with no pastor and local church oversight of their ministry, nor any other ministry connection with their home church other than their membership. This is detrimental to the evangelist and the local church where he attends when he is home. When the evangelist is ministering in other local churches through his ministry, he should serve as a representative of his sending home church. It is biblically incorrect for the evangelist to freelance or work as a free agent in his ministry or to work under the banner of their own name. This is not right. Why?

Sad to say there are local churches and pastors who do not want an evangelist working under the umbrella of their ministry. Why? 1) They don't understand the ministry of the evangelist. 2). the evangelist doesn't understand his/her gift and 3) the evangelist has his or her eyes on being a pastor more than an evangelist and 4) the pastor feel insecure with the evangelist.

This too is absolutely wrong, and shows no respect for the God-gifted evangelist and his work. It must be remembered that the gift of the evangelist is a gift to the local church where God has placed him, and to reject his gift is to reject the Wisdom and Grace of God. The evangelist is an extension of the ministry of his/her pastor and sending local church. Like a missionary, he is commissioned and sent out to others to reach souls for Christ, and assist pastors with the spiritual needs of his people. He directly represents his/her pastor and sending church. As their representative, he/she is also their responsibility.

The evangelist should be part of the pastoral staff. When the evangelist is not actually deployed in the ministry of evangelism, he takes a vibrant part in the ministry (Christian Education, Church Administration, Youth Ministry, Evangelist Outreach and Sick Visitation) of his/her home church, working alongside his pastor for the benefit and blessing of the church family of which he/she is a part.

Today there are few local churches with a God-called, God-gifted evangelist serving out of those churches for the benefit of other local churches of like faith, walk, order, doctrine and discipline. Though God is certainly still calling men and women into this much needed ministry, yet their numbers are fewer than at other time in our history.

The early Church has always had a place for the ministry of evangelism. Without this ministry there has been faltering and decay in our churches and society.

The evangelist sustains a highly important relation to the progress and development of the Church in spiritual life and power.

There are five reasons why the Church cannot afford to suffer the loss of this ministry

1. The evangelist is a gift of Christ to the churches and is not to be despised, rejected, neglected, or unjustly criticized. Their work is just as important in its relationship to the whole program of Christ as the work of the other gifts mentioned...

2. The evangelist is not limited to the work of seeking to win the lost to Christ, but are associated with the other gifted leaders in the work of perfecting the saints unto the work of ministering for the purpose of building up the body of Christ.

3. The evangelist has a divine gift, or perhaps he himself is a divine gift to the churches. He is thus divinely equipped to do a work that no other

church leader can do. The churches need this ministry.

4. The work of the evangelist is not one of self-appointment but, rather, of divine appointment. No man can make himself an evangelist merely by training and experience. Only the risen Christ can give him the gift of an evangelist. Once received, the gift should be developed and used to the limit.

5. The evangelist is God-chosen and Spirit-gifted men/women to lead out in the work of evangelism. They are called by God to inspire pastors, to teach and to lead others in the work of evangelism. Evangelists are Christ's key men/women in His mighty evangelistic program for the world.

CHAPTER FOUR

The Associate Minister as Servant Leader

Associate ministers must recognize that, as servant leaders, the ultimate goal is service. When we are serving others, we are serving God. In *The 21 Irrefutable Laws of Leadership*, John C. Maxwell claims that God deliberately shaped and formed you to serve him in a way that makes your ministry unique.[43] Serving in any capacity in ministry is all about serving God. In *The Soul of Ministry*, Ray S. Anderson asserts that all ministry is grounded in God's ministry, and all theology is dependent on God's continued ministry as the source of revealed truth. To claim a revelation apart from the ministry of God is to violate the first commandment and to clothe ourselves with fig leaves.[44] Any theology that has not been called forth out of God's ministry is shamed based and ends up concealing more than it reveals.

Associate ministers as true servant leaders does all things for God's glory. A servant leader is first and foremost loyal to God, desires to serve others, and is not concerned about serving his or her own interests, manipulating, or seeking personal gain or control. Associate ministers, as servant leaders to God, recognize that service is rendered from their hearts. Maxwell warns that one's heart represents the source of one's motivations.[45] Scripture teaches, "As a face is reflected in water, so the heart reflects the person" (Proverbs 27:19).[46] Maxwell argues that the heart reveals the real person.[47] This is why associate ministers must serve the Lord with all their hearts. How do associate ministers, as servant leaders, know when they are serving God from their hearts? There are two signs that reveal whether or not associate ministers are serving God from the heart: enthusiasm and effectiveness.

Maxwell explains that the first telltale sign of serving God is enthusiasm. When you are doing what you love to do, no one has to motivate you, challenge you, or check up on you. You do not need rewards, applause, or payment, because you love serving in this way.[48] The associate minister as servant leader is shaped by God for serving and meeting the needs of others. These actions define them. They are servant leaders.

According to Maxwell, the second characteristic of serving God from the heart is effectiveness. Whenever you do what God wired you to love to do, you do it well. Passion drives perfection.[49] If you do not care about a task, it is unlikely that you will excel at it. On the other hand, the highest achievers in any field are those who do it because of passion, not duty or profit. Ken Blanchard and Phil Hodges contend that in teaching people to lead like Jesus, we have found that effective leadership starts in the heart. We believe if we do not get the heart right, then we simply will not ever become servant leaders to

God.[50]   God's special servants (called associate ministers) should live in the nature of God, which is with love and compassion. Whenever associate ministers are motivated by self-interest, instead of an interest in serving and meeting the needs of others, they cease to be servant leaders to God. Real servant leaders are always on the lookout for ways to help others.

CHAPTER FIVE

Theological Questions Regarding the Associate Minister

Most Frequently Asked Questions about the Role of the Associate Minister.

Question # 1: What is my role as an associate minister at the church where I serve?

Answer: As an associate minister at the church you have been led by the Holy Spirit to serve actively and cheerfully, your primary role is to support the pastor in his effort to spiritually mature the congregation. This can only be done through your steadfast commitment, faithfulness, and loyalty to the kingdom of God. Remember your pastor must give an account of you, but God will judge you.

Question # 2: What does my certificate of license mean?

Answer: The license that you have been granted gives you the permission under the auspices of the pastor and local church to exercise your gift as you may have opportunity. As a licentiate minister, you are subject to the rules and guidelines of your pastor and church. You must conduct yourself in a manner that would not compromise the gospel and be detrimental to the character and reputation of your pastor and local church.

Question # 3: Should an associate minister participate in worship services, church school, and mid-week bible study?

Answer: As an associate minister at the church where you regularly worship and hold membership, your first responsibility is to be an integral part of the worship experience there. As such, when you are not preaching at another church you are expected by God, the pastor, and congregation to be present at worship. The weekly bible study and church school must not be neglected. Remember you must serve as an example in the church as well as outside of the church.

Question # 4: Now that I am an associate minister, am I expected to tithe?

Answer: Yes, all ministers should and is expected to tithe. Tithing is an act of faith and trust in God. The same God that called you to preach and teach his word expects you to support his church through your giving. Being in a leadership role requires the associate minister to be transparent in the leadership responsibility.

Question # 5: Can a licentiate associate minister perform weddings and funerals?

Answer: An associate minister, if ordained can perform weddings and funerals, but if he is only a licentiate minister, he can not perform weddings, but may participate in funeral or memorial services as designated by his/her pastor.

Question # 6: Does the associate minister's license to preach permit him/her the rights to administer pastoral counseling?

Answer: No, as an associate minister you should not perform any type of counseling in the name of the church unless given permission by the pastor. Your license does not qualify you to administer counseling in the name of the church, unless you have been certified or license by an accredited institution or agency and given permission by your pastor.

Question # 7: What criteria would qualify me for ordination?

Answer: Each church has its own autonomy. Therefore, the rights to ordination are determined by the pastor and the church. Some pastors and churches recognize the completion of seminary training to be merits that would qualify an associate minister for ordination.

Others believe if an associate minister is called to a particular ministry within or outside the church, ordination may be considered or granted. Then, there is the traditional reasoning by pastors and churches for ordination, only if the associate minister is called to a pastorate of a church.

Question #8: What is the difference between the Associate Minister, Assistant to the Pastor, and the Assistant Pastor?

Answer: People of Christian faith are often confused between three of the prominent figures of a congregation, the associate minister, assistant to the pastor and the assistant pastor. Some people use the terms interchangeably, which can cause a false assessment of roles, responsibility, and accountability. Even church members mistake one with the other and most of the time; they are corrected by the said pastor.

The associate minister, technically, is one who has been license by the pastor and church to preach or proclaim the gospel of Jesus Christ. He or she can be ordained to perform specific ministerial duties within and outside the ministry context. They are usually great motivational speakers.

The assistant to the pastor is generally a license and ordained preacher the pastor selects with the approval of the church to assist in the carrying out of pastoral duties. This is not a salary position. The assistant pastor is a salary position. The preacher is called and employed by the pastor and church to function on behalf of the pastor and church. In the pastor's absence he or she carries the same authority as the pastor.

CHAPTER SIX

Ecclesiastical Guidelines for the Associate Minister

Twenty Things Every Associate Minister Needs to Know

1. HAVE A SERVANT'S HEART

The prerequisite of any ministerial service is the heart. If the heart isn't right, nothing will work right. You can fake it for a season, but ultimately who you really are will show up. Every associate minister needs a servant's heart.

Jesus once said to his disciples, you must learn to be servant to all. Not that we should learn to act like servants, but that we should learn to be servants. Servant leaders are made by God. What you do, how you act, and the things you say are a reflection of God and your Christ-like character.

2. DO NOT EXPECT THE PASTOR TO BE YOUR BUDDY

Some associate ministers get upset because they came expecting they would have lunch each day with the pastor, that their families would take outings together and generally speaking, the pastor would be their buddy. God did not call the associate to be the pastor's buddy; he called you to be his helper. Moreover, the pastor is your Spiritual Father.

A true pastor loves and cares for God's people. His burden is to make them the best fed, best loved sheep on earth. The pastor needs help in loving and caring for the sheep. He simply can not spend all his time serving and caring for one sheep. If the pastor wants to hang out with you and be your friend, that's fine, but don't confuse the role of your Spiritual Father and a buddy.

3. IN THE PASTOR'S ABSENCE

People are like sheep. They frighten easily, they are skittish and jittery. The time to make changes in routines is never when the pastor is a way. In his absence, make everything go exactly according to routine. Keep every detail of the worship service exactly as the people are use to. They are already spiritually on the edge because their shepherd is not there with them. Don't add to their anxiety by disrupting their routine or format of doing things. Remember routines are comforting to creatures of habit. When the pastor is away do not fall into the trap of thinking that you are in charge. The pastor is still in charge. The associate minister is there to ensure that things run as if the pastor was there.

4.   BE UNCONDITIONALLY LOYAL

If you can't be loyal to people like your pastor, you can't be loyal to God. In fact, we express our loyalty to God by showing fidelity to others. Your pastor needs someone by his side that will support him, defend him, be true to him and to the vision God has given him with no strings attached. Some associate ministers see their ministry as a stepping stone to being a pastor. Don't build on another man's foundation. Don't seek to take his job for yourself. This is covetousness according to the word of God "Thou shall not covet anything that thou neighbor has." It is also disloyalty and treason, it also dishonors God.

5.   NEVER GOSSIP

Gossip is a sin that most of us feel we are not guilty of and which most of us are very guilty of doing. Gossip may be defined as saying anything negative about the pastor, someone or the ministry. If there are things wrong, take it to the Lord in prayer. Tell absolutely no one, including your spouse. Do not cast aspersion on the character of the pastor or ministry. Doing so dishonors Christ and His cause.

6. DEFEND THE PASTOR AND MINISTRY OF THE CHURCH

As an associate minister you must defend the pastor and the ministry of the church from all negative talk, gossip, slander, and anything that would undermine God's work, as well as the reputation of your pastor. Therefore, if you hear anything even slightly negative about your pastor or about the ministries of the church, intervene, confront, correct and stop it. You must be willing to step into the conversation and boldly rebuke the gossip, thus, replacing it with words of encouragement and a good report. Remember, every church has its critics and its people who think they have a better way of doing things. You must be the eyes and ears of ministry, ever ready to steer the congregants in the right direction.

7. BE AT EVERY SERVICE

A big part of being helpful is being available. You can't help if you aren't there. There are several reasons why you should be at every service if possible.

First, to share the vision and philosophy of ministry; you must be sitting under the same teaching that the congregation is listening to.

Secondly, you need to be fed the word of God. There is no more important time for you to be present than at the church services and Bible studies.

Thirdly, you need to be available to help the pastor where needed. Your primary responsibility is preaching, but when you are not spreading the gospel, you need to help the pastor build up or take care of the congregation at your home church.

Fourthly, you are setting an example for others to follow. If the worship service, Bible study, seminars and meeting are not important for you to attend, why should others attend? People follow your example; they learn by watching you.

8.   HOLD UP YOUR PASTOR'S ARM

As long as Aaron and Hur held up Moses' arms, the battle went well for Israel (Exodus 17:12). Moses needed help, his arms were weary.

Pastors get tired doing God's work and they need someone to hold them up, support and assist them, and lighten their load.

The associate standing minister should be standing by the pastor's side, loving, supporting, praying, and helping him in whatever he deem needed for caring for God's people. Don't create a job for yourself. If you are unhappy move on to serve at another branch of Zion. Never allow self-interest to prevent to you from doing what God called you to do under the authority of the overseer of the flock, which has been appointed by the Holy Spirit.

9. BE SUPPORTIVE AND HELPFUL

To be supportive means to encourage and up-lift the pastor; to bless him; and to strengthen him with prayer, encouraging words, and helpful ideas. To be helpful means to be useful in the details of the ministry, to pick up areas that need to be attended to, and to see them through. Support is an attitude that affects emotions. Help is an action that accomplishes tasks. The pastor needs both help and support.

10. PRAY FOR YOUR PASTOR

As an associate minister of the cloth, you should pray for your pastor every single day and encourage the congregation to do so also, because without prayer, the pastor cannot succeed, with prayer he can not fail. Prayer is the life blood of the ministry. The associate minister should emphasize more prayer and less talk.

11. KEEP CONFIDENTIALITY

Confidentially is vital for a variety of reasons. Confidentially protects the rights and dignity of others. Confidentially protects the church from liability in an age that is quick to sue in court. Absolutely everything that goes on in a ministry is confidential.

Do not ever talk to anyone, including your spouse, about a person's marriage, personal problems, and salaries of church employees, budget considerations, board decisions or anything that is private to a person or family.

Churches have been destroyed by a lack of confidentially. The only exception is that the pastor needs to know everything in order to properly oversee the ministry. The pastor cannot make decisions and oversee the ministry without data. You must be his eyes and ears. In other words, you must be his antenna.

12. BE SUBMISSIVE AND LOYAL

There is a connectedness between submission and loyalty. Therefore, submission is an attitude that continually says, "I'm with you; and I'm on your side; I'm in your corner; I'm pulling for you; I support you; and you can depend on me. Submission means that you can take instructions and follow through on suggestions and directives. It also means since God is going to hold the pastor responsible, the pastor makes the final decisions.

13. STICK TO THE VISION, MISSION, AND PHILOSOPHY OF THE PASTOR

As an associate minister, when you are call to minister or preach to the congregation under the pastor's care, it is your responsibility to know the vision, mission statement and philosophy of ministry of the pastor. You must stick to the vision, mission and philosophy of the pastor by sharing God's word in love and deed.

Remember it's not your vision, mission, and philosophy, but the pastor, therefore don't add to it or take from it by promoting your on agenda or ideology. If God has dreamed his dream in the heart of the pastor, then stick to the vision, mission, and philosophy of ministry of the pastor God has called him to lead and serve his people. Remember he is the angel of the church according to the book of Revelations that God has chosen to be the spokesman to His people.

14. CLEAR EVERYTHING WITH THE PASTOR BEFORE DOING IT

The pastor is the only one in a position to see the big picture (vision) and oversee the entire ministry. He knows what expenditures are coming up and he needs to balance the various aspects of the ministry. He is the one to whom God has given a vision for the overall ministry.

Parenthetically, he is the one who is in a position to navigate and chart the direction of the church priorities and projects. Therefore, before an associate minister make any decision relating to ministry in the church he or she should get clearance from the pastor to line up with the vision, mission statement, and philosophy of ministry of the pastor.

15. DIE TO SELF; AND GET PRIDE OUT OF THE WAY

The associate minister must be in ministry for what he can give, not what he can get. You are in ministry to serve, love, and help others; not for them to serve, love, or help you. You are in the ministry to give, not to get; to care for, not to be cared for.

Therefore, forget your "rights." Forget all the talk about what you deserve. Often associate ministers' feels that they deserve the same benevolence the pastor receives. If he receives gifts from the members I should receive gifts from the members. If someone blesses the pastor monetarily, I should be blessed in the same manner.

This is where we need to die to self and get pride out of the way. Again the associate minister must understand as well as the congregants, his ministry is one of privilege and not entitlement. To preach in the pulpit is a privilege not an entitlement, therefore the associate minister must be grateful whenever the pastor give him/her opportunity to minister through the preaching of God's word.

16. MAKE THE PASTOR LOOK GOOD

Never make the pastor look bad.

This is a basic rule of engagement. Make your pastor look good. There are times when it is necessary to decrease that the pastor may increase. God honors humility. The associate minister must at all cost avoid public criticism of his or her pastor.

Never talk negative with the members about your relationship with the pastor. Always present a united front even if you share in a difference of opinion. Never suggest or tell the congregation that the pastor's ideas are not your ideas. According to scriptures you must be in an agreement, as well as speak the same thing and be on one accord. In other words, there must be a divine connection between the pastor and associate minister.

17. SET THE SPIRITUAL TONE OF THE MINISTRY

The associate minister can be most helpful by making the church a loving, caring place people like to be. Your attitude, friendliness, compassion, concern for others, integrity, and honesty to the lambs and sheep of God sets the tone for ministry.

18. RISE ABOVE PETTY CLIQUES AND DIVISIONS

Every church has them petty cliques and divisions of all sorts. The associate minister must rise above them. The ground at the foot of the cross is flat. God loves all people equally. Jesus is not a respecter of persons. Treat everybody in the Body of Christ or the church equally with love, dignity, and respect. Whether rich or poor; black or white; visitor or regular; or young or old, treat all of God's people to whom Christ died for their sins with kindness. Serve the entire church with loyalty and love. Be true and faithful. Live your life as in the expectancy of the soon to return Lord Jesus Christ.

19. WATCH OUT FOR PEOPLE WITH ULTERIOR MOTIVES

Guard the sheep from wolves in sheep clothing. Watch out for false doctrine, for those who are seeking to divert disciples after themselves. Watch out for those who want to get next to the pastor for promotion and power in the church.

20. DON'T MAKE EXCUSES WHEN CORRECTED

Don't make excuses when you are corrected by your pastor, admit when you are wrong. Some people have a real problem in accepting responsibility with accountability. Remember only what you do for Christ will last.

A Final Word

As I conclude this book, I hope you have a better understanding of the calling and Biblical role of the Associate minister, and a greater desire to do the work of an evangelist. The real truth of who you are can only be revealed in God's Holy Word-The Bible.

Therefore, I charge you to walk worthy of the vocation by which you are called to be God's Servant; doing God's Work, God's Way, by God's Power. Will you answer the call? "Here I am, send me." May God continue to bless your good work.

Bibliography

Anderson, Ray S. The Soul of Ministry. Louisville, KY, Westminister John Knox Press 1997.

Earley, Dave, 21 Reasons Bad Things Happen to Good People. Uhrichsville, Ohio, Barbour Publishing, Inc 2007.

Floyd, Ronnie, 10 Things Every Minister Needs to Know. Green Forest, AR, New Leaf Press, 2006.

Harari and Mukai, A New Decade Demands A New Breed of Managers

Ken Blanchard Ken and Hodges Phil, Lead Like Jesus .Nashville, TN: Thomas Nelson Publishing, 2005.

Maxwell John C, The 21 Irrefutable Laws of Leadership. Nashville, TN: Thomas Nelson Publishers, 1998.

Mckechine, Jean, Webster's New Twentieth Century Dictionary of English Language. Second Edition 1979.

Murray Andrew, Humility: The Beauty of Holiness. Abbotsford, WI: Life Sentence Publishing, 2016.

Nouwen Henri, The Wounded Healer. New York: Doubleday, 1979.

Patterson Ben and Huges Cedar, Mastering the Pastoral Role. Portland, OR, Multnomah Christianity 1991.

Ryle J.C, Expository Thoughts on the Gospels. Volume 2. Grand Rapids, MI: Baker, 2007.

Smith Gordon T, Courage and Calling. Downers, IL. InterVarsity Press, 2011.

Wiersbe, Warren, W. Be Quoted. Grand Rapids MI: Baker Books. 1923.

Wilkes Gene C., Jesus on Leadership: Becoming a Servant Leader. Nashville: TN: Lifeway Press, 2015.

About the Author

A longtime senior executive for the Walt Disney Company, Roy Disney, stated, "It's not hard to make decisions when you know what your values are." This iconic statement can truly provide summation to the spiritual journey of Dr. Bernard P. Goode.

Shortly, after being-called into the gospel ministry, Dr. Goode was mentored by great preachers such as the late Dr. T Wright Morris (past president of Baptist General Convention), the late G.E. Patterson, the presiding bishop of the Church of God in Christ, Dr. A Lincoln James, Jr (Past President of Virginia State Baptist Convention and Vice Pres. National Baptist Convention Congress of Christian Education), Dr. Virgil Woods (Civil Rights Activist/ Martin Luther King, Jr) and Dr. Henry Mitchell (Academic Dean/ Samuel DeWitt Proctor School of Theology).

Dr. Goode decided to further his education in theological studies. He matriculated at the Virginia Commonwealth University, College of Humanities and Science, Trinity Theological Seminary, Virginia University of Lynchburg., Samuel DeWitt Proctor School of Theology (Summa Cum Laude), and South University College of Theology (Summa Cum Laude). He is the recipient of several advance and terminal degrees. Bachelor of Arts/ Religious Studies Degree, Master of Religious Education Degree, Master of Christian Education Degree, Master in Divinity Degree, and three Doctoral Degrees. His doctoral specialization and certification is in Management and Leadership Development, Pastoral Theology and Servant Leadership.

In 2017, he was inducted in the prestigious South University Chapter of the Golden Key International Honor Society for academic excellence and maintaining a 4.0 GPA in the graduate level (Summa Cum Laude). Golden Key is the world's largest collegiate honor society. Membership into the society is by invitation only and applies to the top 15% of college and university sophomores, juniors and seniors, as well as top-performing graduate students in all fields of study, based solely on their academic achievements.

Dr. Goode has distinguished himself by being a Virginia Author through the Library of Congress, Richmond, VA. He is the author of "Pastoral Theology: The Task of the Pastor," "The Calling and Biblical Role of the Associate Minister" and Developing a Servant Leadership Curriculum to Excite, Equip, and Empower Pastor and Church leaders to work together as a Team Ministry. He is an administrator, counselor, mentor, educator, and theologian. He has thirty seven years in ministerial and twenty five years pastoral experience and serve as senior pastor in the residence of Mt. Salem Baptist Church.

Dr. Goode is the President of the Cancer Care Ministry of Caroline and Vicinity (In partnership with Cancer Treatment Center of America). He is a certified Researcher by the National Institutes of Health (NIH) Office of Extramural Research (Certification Number: 12345611). He is a member of Global United Fellowship (GUF), he serves under the spiritual leadership of Honorable Bishop Neil C. Ellis, Presiding Prelate. He also serves as past Global United Fellowship Leader of Christian Education for the Mid-Atlantic Province (churches in the District of Columbia, Maryland, Virginia, and West Virginia). He is a member of South University Doctoral Advisory Council, a member of Robert Greenleaf Center for Servant Leadership, the Virginia Foundation for the Humanities, the American Academy of Religion, Religious Education Association, and the National Museum of African American History and Culture, Washington DC. In addition, he is a past member of the Society of Human Resources Management and past member of the Board of Trustees at Virginia University of Lynchburg.

References

1. Gordon T. Smith, Courage and Calling, (Downers, IL, InterVarsity Press, 2011), 1

2. Ray S. Anderson, The Soul of Ministry, (Louisville, KY, Westminister John Knox Press 1997),

3. Gordon T. Smith, 2.

4. Isaiah 16:7b (KJV)

5. Jn. 12:32, (NIV)

6. 2nd Pet. 1:10 (NIV)

7. Eph. 4:1 (NIV)

8. Lk. 4:18 (NIV)

9. Warren W. Wiersbe, Be Quoted (Grand Rapids, MI, Baker Books, 1923),10.

10. Ibid.

11. Warren W. Wiersbe, Be Quoted (Grand Rapids, MI, Baker Books, 1923), 7.

12. Eph. 6:19-29 (NIV)

13. J.C. Ryle, Expository Thoughts on the Gospels, Volume 2. Grand Rapids, MI: Baker, 2007), 95-96.

14. Andrew Murray, Humility: The Beauty of Holiness (Abbotsford, WI: Life Sentence Publishing, 2016), 3.

15. C. Gene Wilkes, Jesus on Leadership: Becoming a Servant Leader (Nashville: TN: Lifeway Press, 2015), 15.

16. Henri Nouwen, The Wounded Healer (New York: Doubleday, 1979), 5

17. Cedar Hughes and Ben Patterson, Mastering the Pastoral Role, Multnomah Christianity, Publisher, Portland, Or, 1991

18. Hosa 4:6 (NIV)

19. Mt. 28:19-20 (NIV)

20. Jn. 14:26 (NIV)

21. Ronnie Floyd, 10 Things Every Minister Reeds To Know (Green Forest, AR: New Leaf Press, 2006), 107.

22. Prov. 24:27 (NIV)

23. 2nd Cor. 3:6 (NIV)

24. Dave Earley, 21 Reasons Bad Things Happen to Good People (Barbour Publishing, Inc, 2007), 118

25. Ibid, p. 119

26. Rom. 5:20b (KJV)

27. Heb. 11:6 (KJV)

28. Ps. 20:7 (NIV)

29. Jn. 15:5 (BK)

30. James 1:1-4 (KJV)

31. Prov.19:11 (KJV)

32. Habak. 2:3 (KJV)

33. Jere. 29:11 (NIV)

34. Ray S. Anderson, 5.

35. Ibid.

36. Harari and Mukai, A New Decade Demands A New Breed of Managers (Management Review, 1999), 3.

37. Eph 4:11 (NIV).

38. Eph 4:2 (NIV)

39. 2nd Tim 4:5 (NIV)

40. Prov. 29:18 (NIV)

41. Isa. 10:27 (NIV)

42. Lk. 4:18 (NIV)

43. Ibid.

44. Ray S. Anderson, 7.

45. John C. Maxwell, The 21 Irrefutable Laws of Leadership (Nashville, TN: Thomas Nelson Publishers, 1998), 127.

46. Prov. 27:19 (ECV).

47. Maxwell, 128.

48. Ibid., 236.

49. Ibid., 237.

50. Ken Blanchard and Phil Hodges, Lead Like Jesus (Nashville, TN: Thomas Nelson Publishing, 2005), 39.

CPSIA information can be obtained
at www.ICGtesting.com
Printed in the USA
LVHW021502071019
633402LV00008B/3625/P